Table of Contents

Confessions of a Child Predator
An Interview with a Convicted Child Predator That
Caused the Death of Five Teenagers
©Copyright 2013 by Harry Jay

DISCLAIMER AND TERMS OF USE AGREEMENT:

(Please Read This Before Using This Book)
This information is for educational and informational purposes only. The content is not intended to be a substitute for any professional advice, diagnosis, or treatment.

The authors and publisher of this book and the accompanying materials have used their best efforts in preparing this book.

The authors and publisher make no representation or warranties with respect to the accuracy, applicability, fitness, or completeness of the contents of this book. The information contained in this book is strictly for educational purposes. Therefore, if you wish to apply

Introduction – Keep a Diligent Watch

Hi, I'm Dr. Harry Jay, Chief Research Scientist for Applied Mind Sciences http://appliedmindsciences.com.

Applied Mind Sciences is a mind research think tank located in Southern Utah. We conduct studies of the mind; how it operates, what influences it and more.

In 2006, a child predator using by the moniker of Johnny B Goode began a reign of terror perpetrated solely against teenagers frequenting chat rooms.

My colleague, Dr. Leland Benton, Chief Forensics Investigator for ForensicsNation http://forensicsnation.com called me halfway through the investigation to profile the perpetrator.

After reviewing the chat room transcripts and all of the information that Dr. Benton provided, I determined that the perpetrator was not a man but a woman posing as a man.

As I read the chat room transcripts I quickly became alert over the fact that the way the perpetrator articulated her conversations, the nurturing tones, and the high level of concern and caring, led me quickly to determine that this was not a man but a woman.

And I was right and wrong!

It turned out that the perpetrator was not a woman but two women – a mother and daughter team.

In the course of the two month investigation that ensued to catch this child predator team, I worked closely with the ForensicsNation's team of investigators as they literally tracked the perpetrator(s) down and finally had both women arrested but not until they had caused the death of 5-teenagers.

I should warn you in advance that men are more often the perpetrators of child predation and not women.

This was a very unusual case in many regards as you shall see as you read through the interview transcripts.

What follows first is the synopsis of the investigation that I took from the log files at ForensicsNation and then a personal interview I conducted with the convicted child predators themselves.

Be advised that the names, the time stamps, and locations have been changed by agreement between me and the child predators in order to have access to the interview.

Synopsis: Child Predators

Case File Number 200608-001-FN-6

In August 2006 a woman, under the moniker of Johnny B Goode, began accessing teen chat rooms and posing as a young male teenager. Over an 8-month period, she was responsible for 5-teen suicide deaths caused by cyber-bullying. Law Enforcement was unable to determine her identity or her location. She operated through a series of offshore proxies based in China and then only through computers she hijacked effectively hiding her identity and location. ForensicsNation was hired by one of the parents of the victims to hunt this stalker down and bring him/her to justice. What follows is a synopsis of how the perpetrator(s) were hunted down putting an end to their reign of terror.

*****

August 8, 2206 – retained for the case.

August 11, 2006 – contacted the 5-chat rooms where Jonny B Goode was registered and where all 5-victims had met her. All 5-chat rooms agreed to cooperate in catching the Suicide Stalker.

August 12, 2006 – Installed ForensicsNation software probe code named "Newman". Newman is a virtual watch dog that plants itself inside any computer system or network (we will not tell you how or where) and sits and watches silently. When a hacker or intrusion of any kind is detected by Newman, it plants itself inside the perpetrator's computer and watches to see what other cyber-crimes the perpetrator is committing as it begins to gather evidence. Newman can break through any proxy, and defense that a perpetrator attempts to hide behind and deliver the evidence to ForensicsNation to eventually be turned over to law enforcement. To date, Newman has never been defeated. You can run but you cannot hide because Newman will find you no matter what it takes.

August 13, 2006 – Newman reports a target and in the process of sending data the perpetrator shuts down her computer. This is highly perplexing; Newman has never been discovered since Newman disguises himself as a .dll file extension and is not visible to even the best anti-virus and spyware programs but the facts speak for themselves. The ForensicsNation team assembles to discuss what could have happened. In the course of the discussion two facts emerge: 1) the perpetrator is a highly skilled computer person. 2) The perpetrator must have been watching her outbound bandwidth transmission and discovered something was communicating outbound so she shut the computer down.

August 14, 2006 – taking into consideration that the perpetrator knows that she has been penetrated, we continue to watch the 5-known chat rooms while ForensicsNation investigators make contact with 12-other well know teen chat rooms and explain the investigation to them. All of them with the exception of one chat room agree to allow ForensicsNation to scan their operations on a 24/7 basis. Newman is installed on all 11-chat rooms and programmed NOT to communicate back to ForensicsNation except at start-up when the perpetrator turns her computer on and then only in a burst transmission which takes about a nanosecond. If the perpetrator is watching, she will not be able to see any outbound activity.

August 16, 2006 – After scanning all chat rooms for over 48-hours, ForensicsNation determines that the perpetrator is not a registered member under another name. At this point, all efforts are directed to new member registrations. ForensicsNation personnel begin scanning all new member registrations dating back to August 13, 2006.

August 18, 2006 – ForensicsNation personnel discover a new registration under the moniker "FreakyB" is using the same offshore proxy setup as Johnny B Goode. Newman is programmed to penetrate FreakyB when she next signs on.

August 22, 2006 – ForensicsNation personnel begin to become concerned that somehow FreakyB has discovered she is being monitored but since Newman has not made a penetration because she has not signed on, ForensicsNation personnel sit patiently and wait.

August 24, 2006 – Newman reports a target when FreakyB signs on to one of the chat rooms and immediately goes to sleep and lays dormant. ForensicsNation personnel monitor FreakyB's activities as she engages numerous teens in a chat. After 16-minutes, FreakyB signs off.

August 28, 2006 – Newman transmits in a burst transmission the IP-address and location of the perpetrator's computer and then immediately shuts down. Perpetrator's computer is located in Falls Church, VA. Newman determines that perpetrator is using an air card issued by Verizon under the name of Stanley Kidderman

9

but at a different address in Suffolk, VA. Law Enforcement officials are notified and both jurisdictions send out detectives to both addresses. Two facts emerge from the detective's reports: 1) Stanley Kidderman is a retired fireman with lung disease and was not aware that his air card was lost or stolen. His live-in nurse stated that he is an active computer user and the detectives asked if he would voluntarily submit to having his computer searched. Kidderman grants his permission. Subsequent investigation of the Kidderman computer by law enforcement analysts revealed that Kidderman was not the perpetrator. 2) The Church Falls address belonged to a Mrs. Carl Knudsen, a widower and pensioner that rarely uses her computer but leaves it on 24/7. Mrs. Knudsen also consented to a voluntary computer search and it was determined that the Knudsen computer had been hijacked. To ForensicsNation personnel, the perpetrator is hijacking computers to remain hidden. It is also obvious to ForensicsNation personnel that the perpetrator is one smart cookie and takes no chances. With the consent by both Kidderman and Knudsen, Newman is installed on both computers.

September 3, 2006 – Newman transmits a new target with an IP-address and location in Norfolk, VA. Follow-up investigation by ForensicsNation personnel reveals the same scenario – a hijacked computer.

September 11, 2006 – all activity by FreakyB in the aforementioned chat rooms has ceased. Newman has not reported any new target for over a week. The ForensicsNation team assembles to discuss this new development. It is obvious that subsequent to both investigations of the Kidderman and Knudsen computers, the perpetrator has become aware of law enforcement zeroing in on her activities. This could explain the sudden cessation of FreakyB activities. The mystery remains on how perpetrator found out about law enforcement's actions.

September 12, 2006 – ForensicsNation's sister company – Applied Mind Sciences – sends a behavioral scientist, Dr. Harry Jay, to profile the perpetrator. After reviewing all chat room logs and communications, the AMS doctor determines that the perpetrator is a woman disguised as a young teenage boy.

September 13, 2006 – the ForensicsNation team assembles and determines that Kidderman's live-in nurse is now a viable suspect. She was present at the time detectives made their inquiry of Kidderman. A call is made to Kidderman requesting the nurse's cell phone number. At this time Kidderman reveals that he owns the cell phone and pays the monthly bill but has never used the phone. He gives permission for ForensicsNation personnel, to place a laser GPS tag on the phone and ForensicsNation personnel begin scanning past text messages and call patterns.

September 15, 2006 – ForensicsNation's investigation of the nurse's cell phone revealed the following: 1) She conducted very few text messaging and only to her children. 2) The majority of her cell phone voice calls were to businesses providing services to Kidderman with very few personal calls. 3) There were two calls made to toll free numbers for periods over 20-minutes. 4) Investigation of these toll-free numbers using a toll-free number owner identifier reveals that both numbers were to computer dial-up companies. Because of what the investigation revealed, Kidderman's nurse is now the prime suspect.

September 17, 2006 – FreakyB reappears in one of the chat rooms. ForensicsNation personnel immediately conduct a scan Kidderman nurse's cell phone to see if it is in use. It is not but the scan also reveals that the phone is turned off and the battery removed since the GPS function is not working completely. Note: a cell phone's GPS can be turned off from the cell phone's menu but not completely. The GPS function will still remain available for emergency services. The only way to completely turn off a cell phone's GPS is to remove the battery. Newman once again transmits new target info and again after subsequent investigation, it is another hijacked computer.

September 18, 2006 – ForensicsNation personnel question Kidderman again about the whereabouts of his nurse at the time of FreakyB coming online. Kidderman informed ForensicsNation personnel that his nurse had the day off and was not present in his home. Kidderman was not aware of her whereabouts on any of her days off but confirmed that she leaves for the day and doesn't return until the following morning.

September 19, 2006 - ForensicsNation team assembles to discuss the latest developments. There is now no doubt in any of the team member's mind that Kidderman's nurse is FreakyB. Team members make contact with Kidderman and again request permission to place a GPS tracking tag on the nurse's cell phone. Kidderman grants permission and a laser tag is placed on the phone. Note: a laser tag is placed by calling the target phone number and marrying the tag to the phone even if the phone is not answered.

September 20, 2006 – Kidderman confirms that his nurse's next day off is September 23rd.

September 23, 2006 – Kidderman's nurse departs for her day off. She is tracked to the public library four blocks away from Kidderman's home. Immediately FreakyB signs on to one of chat rooms. Law enforcement is called in and sent immediately to nurse's location. Nurse is detained and the library's computer is confiscated as evidence.

September 24, 2006 - ForensicsNation team receives a call from law enforcement personnel that an analysis of the library's computer reveals that the nurse was not online with a chat room as FreakyB but was online on Skype chatting with her daughter. Nurse is released without being charged. ForensicsNation team assembles to discuss this amazing development. If Kidderman's nurse is not FreakyB then who is? And how can it be explained that FreakyB logged on to the chat room at the exact same time the nurse was chatting with her daughter? Suspicion is now cast on the daughter and the team orders an investigation of the daughter.

September 25, 2006 – ForensicsNation personnel make contact with Kidderman and request any information about the nurse's daughter. Kidderman is of no help and does not know the daughter nor has he ever met her. A search of the daughter's Skype registration information reveals only that she lives in Atlanta, GA and her first name is Francine. A check of Skype's computer logs reveals an Atlanta, GA IP-Address and the cable carrier that provided ISP services to the daughter. A further check of the ISP's data files reveals the daughter's first and last name, her home address and her occupation – COMPUTER PROGRAMMER FOR IBM.

September 27, 2006 – ForensicsNation team members make contact with IBM security personnel and request permission to place Newman on her office computer. IBM security personnel are highly doubtful that daughter would use her work station to commit cyber-stalking but grants permission. Note: Throughout the investigation all times and log-ons for FreakyB show that a good majority of them were during business hours where suspect would be at work. This fact alone was enough to sway IBM security personnel to allow Newman.

September 29, 2006 – Librarian at the library that nurse was using to talk to daughter on Skype notifies ForensicsNation team that the nurse has just logged on to another library computer. ForensicsNation team checks and immediately sees that FreakyB logs in to one of the chat rooms. Newman reports a target identifying daughter's work station communication with library computer using Skype and also logged into chat room. We got her. The perpetrator is the daughter. ForensicsNation team notifies IBM security and law enforcement and daughter is arrested and her computer confiscated.

September 30, 2006 – While under interrogation daughter reveals that her mother participated in the stalking. Nurse/mother is arrested.

Case Closed October 2, 2006.

Follow-Up

In December 2007 both perpetrators were convicted at trial in the Federal District of New York (it is federal because of crossing state lines) of (charges have been omitted by mutual consent but you can assume the "book" was thrown at them) and are now serving life sentences in Federal Prison.

Interview

I conducted the interview at the Federal Bureau of Prisons USP Hazelton, WV the bureau's only maximum security facility for women. I will use the terms CP1 for the daughter and CP2 for the mother.

DHJ: Ladies, you know who I am since I testified at your trial. My purpose today is to ask questions in order to better understand the mindset of child predators and to add to the research my company, Applied Mind Sciences, is engaged in to assist in treatment of child predators. So, to begin...

CP1: What makes you think we are sick?

CP2: I think it is presumptuous on your part to assume we are sick.

DHJ: I think it should be taken as a given that causing the death of 5-teenagers is cause for the mental health community to label child predation as a disease.

CP2: I consider that still presumption on your part but for the record, my daughter and I do not believe we are suffering from any mental illness. And the evidence presented at trial was all circumstantial. Not once was any evidence presented that showed my daughter and I actually committing any of the charges.

DHJ: Ladies, 12-jurors deliberated for less than 30-minutes and came back to return a unanimous verdict of guilty. It doesn't matter what either of you think; enough evidence was presented to cause a guilty verdict.

CP1: And next you are going to tell us that there aren't any innocent people in prison, right? You are not concerned with one thing my mother said; all you are concerned with is documenting our "illness" in order for you to make a name for yourself as helping to put away two famous child predators.

DHJ: Ladies, first of all the proper term is "infamous" and not famous and second of all, by agreement, my company has worked out an arrangement with the Federal Bureau of Prisons to place money on the books for you to use that is outside the scope of your restitution and judgment. Now, if you ladies are going to be combative and continue with this line of inane reasoning then I will stop the interview and rescind our arrangement. Is this understood?

CP2: I guess you have us both backed into a corner…so let's just get this over with so we can leave.

DHJ: Better! Now, tell me exactly why you did this and, what in your mind caused you to commit these crimes.

CP2: Speaking for myself, I have always felt that teenagers today are just a plain waste of human flesh. They are all spoiled, talk trash, do drugs and sex and are just no good. They do poorly in school and use school as just a social meet up. As far as I'm concerned, the whole lot of them should be removed.

DHJ: By removed, do you mean exterminate them? All of them?

CP2: Exactly; call it whatever you wish.

DHJ: You have personally met every teenager in the world, right?

CP2: Now look who is talking silly. Of course I haven't met EVERY teenager and I am talking in generalities.

DHJ: The Nazis held the same beliefs against the Jews. Do you think this was right too?

CP1: You are putting words into my mother's mouth. What Hitler did was extermination; what we did was justice.

DHJ: Justice for what?

16

CP1: Justice for everyone not having to tolerate teenage aggression, teenage crime and teenage sex antics anymore.

DHJ: Listen ladies; let's assume for a minute that you are right; that all teenagers deserve to die. How could the two of you expect to do any good against the millions of teenagers in this country alone?

CP2: We didn't expect to get caught so quickly and we expected to rally other people to our cause by using and manipulating the press.

CP1: Yeah, there are others that feel the same way we do; we aren't the only ones that think teenagers are a waste.

DHJ: How long have you ladies held these beliefs and where did they come from?

CP2: My daughter was a victim of date rape when she was 15-years old. The boy just laughed at me and my daughter and said he would be back for some more "sugar." My daughter and I have been alone since she was born. I don't know who the father was…

DHJ: We will get to the father part in just a moment…so you were one of those same teenagers experimenting with sex and got pregnant. So you deserve to die too?

CP2: No, I too was raped and never knew who did it. I didn't "experiment" with sex nor did I do drugs or carry on with what teenagers do today. My parents would not allow such behavior.

CP1: My mother wouldn't allow me to carry on either. I never have taken drugs, nor do I smoke or go partying.

DHJ: (To the mother) Why haven't you ever told your daughter who her father is? And for the record, was your daughter really raped or did you set it up to look like a rape.

17

CP2: That information is confidential and I demand to know how you got access to it! And yes, my daughter was raped…how dare you…

DHJ: I have access to all investigation and trial transcripts. You may have given the information to a court psychologist but it is not subject to confidentiality. I will ask you again; why haven't you ever revealed to your daughter the identity of her father and how is it, as controlling an influence that you are in your daughter's life that you even allowed her to date let alone be raped?

CP2: This interview is over and you can shove your money. I want out of here…NOW! I don't have to put up with your stupid questions.

CP1: Momma, what is he talking about? You know who my dad is?

CP2: Shut your mouth and remain quiet. I will handle this. Like I said, this interview is over and I demand for my daughter and me to be taken back to our cells.

DHJ: Sorry ladies, it doesn't work that way. Please read the agreement. I am free to ask any question I choose. Understand I know more than your daughter and I find it highly doubtful that you would allow her to date the very same young men that you despise. Sorry, it doesn't add up so in my mind, the only reason you allowed this was to set up some unsuspecting young man in some kind of trap.

CP2: (Screaming) Don't you dare tell my daughter a thing…do you hear me…not a thing! And you can believe anything you want. The facts are the facts…

DHJ: I'm not going to tell your daughter anything but you are.

CP1: Momma, what is he talking about?

CP2: I told you to be quiet and not say a word.

CP1: I am not a child mother and I won't remain quiet. Now do you know who my daddy is?

CP2: Yes, but I have always believed it is better that you don't know.

CP1: Why? Who gives you the right to withhold important information from me? I want to know who my daddy is.

DHJ: Listen; what you have done is withhold information from your daughter and I can understand why but she has a right to know and you need to do the right thing.

CP2: She never would have known if you didn't bring it up and violate my privacy.

DHJ: What about the 5-teenagers you violated. They don't have any privacy any more. You gave up your right to privacy when you were convicted in a court of law.

CP2: Words! You are a master of words but what you fail to understand is we don't care about your world and your rules. We live and play by our rules and in my world you don't have a right to disrupt my family.

DHJ: Ah, we are now getting to the crux of the matter. You have your own world that you live in…your own fantasy?

CP2: It is no fantasy; it is as real as mud.

DHJ: But it only exists in your mind and possibly your daughter's mind.

CP2: No, it exists in quite a few people's minds that think the youth in this country is going to hell…

CP1: Don't try to change the subject, momma; I want to know who my daddy is?

Long silence…

DHJ: Go ahead; we can wait…and as far as hell is concerned, I think it is safe to say that there is a very special place reserved for you in hell.

CP2: I am not saying another word and I really don't give a damn what you think!

DHJ: Then our deal is off and the both of you can rot in this prison until they carry you both out in a box.

CP1: Tell me momma or I will them him of all the others we killed.

CP2: I told you to be quiet…

CP1: I will not be quiet…

CP2: SHUT YOUR MOUTH NOW!

CP1: NO! YOU ARE GOING TO TELL ME OR SO HELP ME I WILL THEM HIM EVERYTHING, MOMMA!

Prevailing silence…

CP1: My mother and I killed the boy who raped me. It wasn't rape! The first time was consensual. The second time, I lured him into our house and my mother hit him with a hammer until he was dead. We then cut up his body and put the pieces into plastic trash bags and buried the remains randomly around the county. Then we…

CP2: (in a rage CP2 attacks her daughter knocking over the interview table) I TOLD YOU TO KEEP QUIET (prison officials pour into the room and subdue both women and take them back to their cells.

I returned after 5-days to continue the interview. The two women had been placed in solitary confinement and this was the first time that they had seen each other since the last interview. Present in the interview room were two female correction officers.

DHJ: I hope we do not have a repeat of the incident we had in our last session. Both of you are free to tell me anything and since you are already serving a life sentence, I see little harm in revealing any other crimes that you have committed. You will never leave prison and I expect complete honestly so let's begin again...

CP2: Nothing has changed; I do not want my family's privacy violated and I will not tolerate you or anyone else revealing things that are best left alone...

DHJ: You don't get it, do you? You have no rights and cannot dictate any terms whatsoever in this interview. You are a convicted felon serving a life sentence and for the rest of your life will do what you are told or remain in solitary confinement. Now, you can cooperate and make it easy for you and your daughter or you can be combative and pay the price but you have no control whatsoever in this interview.

CP2: You are really enjoying this, aren't you? You enjoy dominance over women and you can sit there and wonder why we decide to kill men like you?

DHJ: First of all, you killed teenage boys and not men; boys that were naïve and not careful. You used sex to lure them into your web of deceit. You took advantage of their naivety and youth. I am not a teenage boy, nor do I take any pleasure in dominating anyone. This interview has one expressed goal; to determine all of the facts so we can prevent situations like the ones that you and your daughter caused from occurring again.

CP2: Interesting speech but you still enjoy your dominance over my daughter and me...

HJS: You seem to have a problem with understanding words and word associations. In the case of your daughter and you the word "dominance" is appropriate since you chose to murder five young boys and take their lives. That is dominance! This interview and the prison officials charged with your incarceration are not attempting to dominate you; the proper word is control...

CP2: Like I said before, you are a master of words but in my mind control and dominance are the same.

DHJ: Yes, I know and at last you are being truthful but the two words have different definitions. Dominance means the disposition of an individual to assert control in dealing with others while control means to hold in check. Candidly, I think what we are discussing is part of your problem. You confuse words and their meanings and these confusions cause you to do things that are wrong.

CP2: I'm no scholar but I do know the definitions of words.

DHJ: Really? In our first interview you claimed that what the Nazis did was exterminate but what you did was justice. But you both did the same thing; you killed innocent people.

CP2: Innocent...innocent you say? Rape is not innocent.

DHJ: By your daughter's own admission in our last session, there was no rape. What you and your daughter did was premeditated murder.

CP2: It became premeditated only after the injustices that were committed against us.

DHJ: Injustices for what? In our first session you claimed that society should have to tolerate teenage aggression, teenage crime and teenage sex antics anymore. I will agree that you were raped but your daughter was not. In fact, your daughter admitted that the sex was consensual. Isn't it true that you cooked up these crimes and involved your daughter in order to alleviate whatever trauma or anxiety was caused by you being raped? But it is more than that; isn't it?

CP2: What do you mean?

DHJ: The fact is that you hate your daughter and have always hated your daughter.

CP2: I don't hate my daughter; I have done my best to protect her.

DHJ: Protect her from what?

CP2: From men...boys that just want to use her for sex.

DHJ: Use her? By her own admission the sex was consensual. Nobody used anybody. She wanted to have sex just like the boy.

CP2: She was young; she didn't know better.

DHJ: Okay, I will agree with that but there are other cases of young women engaging in teenage sex and their parents don't plot to kill the boys. But because of your hate for your daughter, you decided to murder young boys.

CP2: You keep saying I hate my daughter and I do not.

DHJ: Come now; let's look at the facts. When you discovered you were pregnant from the rape you attempted on three occasions to get an abortion. The clinics you consulted are required by law back then to log all contact...

CP2: How dare you invade my privacy again; I told you...

DHJ: Sit down and be quiet or these two correction officers will restrain you. We are not going to have a repeat of the first session. To continue, when you could get an abortion you attempted suicide...

CP1: Why couldn't my mother get an abortion?

DHJ: Back then, she needed her parent's consent and she couldn't get the consent so she was turned away.

CP1: Mom, why didn't your parents consent to the abortion? (Mother is silent)

23

DHJ: The reason is because your grandfather is your father. Your mother was raped by her father.

CP2: Bastard…you are a bastard…

CP1: So this is all true; you hate me because I ruined your life even though I didn't cause the rape. And because you hate me, you decided to involve me in this stupid scheme of yours to pay me back. It never had anything to do with the boys; this was always about me?

CP2: Don't listen to what he is saying; he is just trying to break up our relationship…don't you see?

CP1: What relationship is there to break up, mom? We are in prison for life. What he is saying is true; you have always hated me and now because of this hate you decided to create a "cause" in order to justify murder. Why didn't you report grandpa for what he had done?

DHJ: Your grandfather died of mysterious circumstances soon after you were born.

CP1: Tell me something, mother…did you murder my grandfather too?

CP2: What benefit is there asking these questions when what is done is done?

CP1: Did you kill my grandfather? Answer me, mother!

CP2: Yes…yes dammit…I poisoned the sick asshole for what he did to me for eight long years and I would do it again if I had to and you would too. Don't you judge me; you didn't suffer from the abuse.

CP1: I beg to differ, mother; you suffered for eight years and now I have a life sentence because of your sickness.

CP2: It's not the same…

CP1: No, it is not the same; I'm condemned to die in prison thanks to you. You must really hate me, mother.

CP2: I don't hate you; I love you. I just wanted to protect you from what happened to me.

24

CP1: No mother; there is no love in you. We killed those boys; we snuffed out their lives and some they don't even know about of which I will tell them. You are living in some kind of fantasy where you have convinced yourself that you are something you are not. I see all of this now...how could you, mother?

CP2: Believe what you want but I do love you and that is no fantasy. Teenage crime statistics speak for themselves; they are all sick just like my father.

CP1: So who are you to determine who should live and who should die?

CP2: Shut up...shut your mouth. Who are you to question me?

DHJ: Shut up? Are you still trying to control your daughter and control everything?

CP2: You can shut up too; I am sick of all of this. You have destroyed my family and what little I have left in this world...

DHJ: No, you have destroyed it; not me. You are the person accountable for all of this. You lived a lie and you included your daughter in this lie so you shut up and accept what you have done.

CP2: You didn't need to reveal all of this to my daughter; she is not better off knowing all of this.

CP1: Yes, mother, I am better off because it opened my eyes to the truth. Don't you see what we have done? Don't you see how your hatred caused all of this? Okay, grandpa raped you and he is also my father. Is this the end of the world? Those boys we killed didn't have anything to do with it. You took out your hatred on them and you used me. Okay, I went along with it because I thought you were right at the time and now I am paying the price. But at least I know I did wrong and I am not hiding behind some sick façade.

CP2: Oh, don't you talk down to me as if you are holier than thou all of a sudden. You enjoyed killing those boys as much as I did.

CP1: Enjoyed, mother? Why do you think I enjoyed killing those boys? It seems to me after each murder that you had to console me for days.

CP2: That was all just an act on your part to get attention so I went along with it.

CP1: An act, mother? If I didn't do what you said you would fly into a rage and start hitting me. I see now that you became an abuse because you were abused but that excuse your rage.

CP2: You are beginning to sound like this doctor. All of a sudden you have an epiphany? I don't buy it; it is all just another act on your part.

CP1: Believe what you want mother but take a good long last look at me; I don't ever want to see you again or have anything to do with you again.

Interview was terminated.

Conclusions

The interview with CP1 and CP2 was difficult for me.

Most cases involving crimes against children are perpetrated by men and not women.

Statistics show that the norm is changing as more and more women are committing crimes against children.

As I write this, Applied Mind Sciences is only one group that is studying this phenomenon.

The court barred the women from receiving any financial gain for selling their story to the media.

All monies would first be applied to their court-ordered restitution.

I applied for and was granted a special dispensation in the name of scientific research.

I have two daughters and I am a widower.

Parents live in a state of constant fear that some predator is out there lurking to ensnare them in some type of evil intent.

Let us not forget that the first grave ever dug was for a son if you recall the story of Cain and Abel in the bible.

We live in an evil world and only the dedication of law enforcement and groups such as ForensicsNation stand in battle against the ever increasing cyber-criminals.

I can only assist them; sometimes a person wants to do more.

It doesn't take a trained behavioral scientist to see through the veil of rot in these two women's mind.

All mentally ill people deny they are sick and all hide behind some false sense of justification for their actions.

They speak in generalities but the targets of their crimes are not general albeit specific.

As with most depravity, a person spirals down from one depravity to the next while each downward spiral is worse than the one before it.

CP2's father was never prosecuted for his crime; he died of mysterious circumstances soon after CP1 was born and as reveled in the interview CP2 murdered her own father by slowly poisoning him.

CP1 grew up without ever knowing that her grandfather was her father.

When the daughter grew up and they both started "baiting" young boys, the spiral became more intense.

Their first victim was the daughter's lover.

The gruesome details of how they killed this young man will stay with me for a long time.

The killing became habitual; all directed against teenage boys because all teenage boys represented the evil in these women's minds as defined by the mother.

The power over these young men soon became addictive to these women and they couldn't and wouldn't stop their evil deeds.

I am not going to employ any psycho-babble regarding my findings from this interview.

My intention is to spare you the boring stuff.

But I do want you to take away from this book a few things.

First, watch your children and watch them hard.

Know where they are and what they are doing.

Check their rooms and their computers to see what is occupying their time.

Know their friends, where they hangout and keep in close contact with their school administrations.

Second, talk to your children daily.

Question them on what they have been doing and what they have been learning.

Question them about their friends, their acquaintances and if anything odd has been happening in their lives.

Look for drug abuse in their eyes, the quality of their hair and skin and teeth.

Drugs have devastating effects on the human body and leave telltale signs.

One of our company divisions – SurvivalNations – has an interesting product that I purchased for my two daughters as well as myself.

It is a GPS device that can track your children's movements at all times and it provides an Internet interface where you can dial in and know their exact location.

Follow-up:

Since our interview, CP1 has not spoken to her mother.

She requested and was granted a change in cells out of the cell block where her mother resides.

She wrote me a letter a few weeks after the interview detailing the additional murders of 11-more boys, which I turned over to law enforcement.

At the time of this writing, the authorities are deciding whether to charge both women with the additional murders.

CP1 asked me to stay in touch with her but one thing stood out in her letter that caused me to wonder and be cautious.

She asked if I could find a way for her to speak to children through letters to warn them of the dangers lurking out there.

She wanted to become the voice of caution.

I am looking into this for her; but I AM SUSPICIOUS THAT CP1 HAS HAD A COMPLETE TUNR AROUND SO QUICKLY.

Her mother may be right; it is all an act and I will watch her closely.

It may all become an exercise in futility since the Federal Bureau of Prisons has to agree to this so we will have to wait and see.

If it is done, it will have to be done by letters and possibly audio and video.

I sincerely hope that this book results in parents exercising more control and attention over their kids.

Statistics - Female Sex Offenders - Female Sexual Predators

75% of sexual predators are male and **25% are female**.

86% of the victims of female sexual predators aren't believed, so the crimes go unreported and don't get prosecuted.

The American Humane Association which was responsible for gathering data from the yearly reports provided by the 50 U.S. states child protective agencies from 1973 through 1987 on child sexual abuse.

They found that approximately 20 percent of substantiated cases of child sexual abuse during that time period had been perpetrated by females

According to David Finkelhor, director of the Crimes Against Children Research Center at the University of New Hampshire, U.S.A. and stated in one of the largest newspapers in the U.S.A., the rise in recognition and prosecution of female sexual predators is due at least in part to the increased number of female police officers.

Apparently, this results in prosecution of female sexual predators for their crimes without the police being labeled misogynistic.

From the Health Canada report of 1996

The Invisible Boy

Revisioning the Victimization of Male Children and Teens

Female Perpetrators

As recently as 10 years ago, it was a common assumption that females did not or could not sexually abuse children or youth.

Even some professionals working in the field believed that women represented only about 1% to 3% of sexual abusers at most.

However, mounting research evidence about sexual abuse perpetration at the hands of teen and adult females has begun to challenge our assumptions, though these earlier and dated views still tend to predominate.

The percentage of women and teenage girl perpetrators recorded in case report studies is small and ranges from 3% to 10% (Kendall-Tackett and Simon, 1987; McCarty, 1986; Schultz and Jones, 1983; Wasserman and Kappel, 1985).

When the victim is male, female perpetrators account for 1 % to 24% of abusers.

When the victim is female, female perpetrators account for 6% to 17% of abusers (American Humane Association, 1981; Finkelhor and Russell, 1984; Finkelhor et al., 1990).

In the Ontario Incidence Study, 10% of sexual abuse investigations involved female perpetrators (Trocme, 1994).

However, in six studies reviewed by Russell and Finkelhor, female perpetrators accounted for 25% or more of abusers. Ramsay-Klawsnik (1990) found that adult females were abusers of males 37% of the time and female adolescents 19% of the time.

Both of these rates are higher than the same study reported for adult and teen male abusers.

Dynamics of Female-Perpetrated Abuse

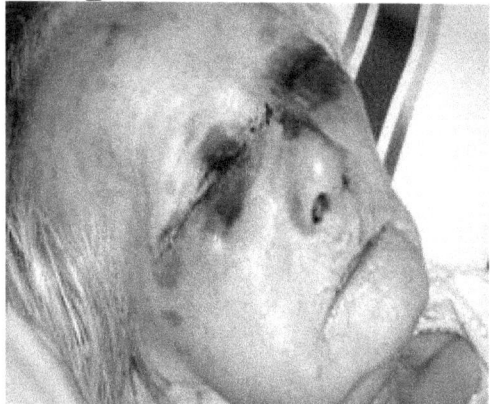

Some research has reported that female perpetrators commit fewer and less intrusive acts of sexual abuse compared to males.

While male perpetrators are more likely to engage in anal intercourse and to have the victim engage in oral-genital contact, females tend to use more foreign objects as part of the abusive act (Kaufman et al., 1995).

This study also reported that differences were not found in the- frequency of vaginal intercourse, fondling by the victim or abuser, genital body contact without penetration or oral contact by the abuser.

Females may be more likely to use verbal coercion than physical force.

The most commonly reported types of abuse by female perpetrators include vaginal intercourse, oral sex, fondling and group sex (Faller, 1987; Hunter et al., 1993).

However, women also engage in mutual masturbation, oral, anal and genital sex acts, show children pornography and play sex games (Johnson, 1989; Knopp and Lackey, 1987).

The research suggests that, overall, female and male perpetrators commit many of the same acts and follow many of the same patterns of abuse against their victims.

They also do not tend to differ significantly in terms of their relationship to the victim (most are relatives) or the location of the abuse (Allen, 1990; Kaufman et al., 1995).

It is interesting to note in the study by Kaufman et al. (1995) that 8% of the female perpetrators were teachers and 23% were babysitters, compared to male perpetrators who were 0% and 8% respectively.

Finkelhor et al. (1988) also report significantly higher rates of sexual abuse of children by females in day-care settings.

Of course, Finkelhor's findings should not surprise us given that women represent the majority of day-care employees.

Research on teen and adult female sexual abuse perpetrators has found that many suffer from low self-esteem, antisocial behavior, poor social and anger management skills, fear of rejection, passivity, promiscuity, mental health problems, post-traumatic stress disorder and mood disorders (Hunter et al., 1993; Mathews, Matthews and Speltz, 1989).

However, as in the case of male perpetrators, research does not substantiate that highly emotionally disturbed or psychotic individuals predominate among the larger population of female sexual abusers (Faller, 1987).

There is some evidence that females are more likely to be involved with co-abusers, typically a male, though studies report a range from 25% to 77% (Faller, 1987; Kaufman et al., 1995; McCarty, 1986).

However, Mayer (1992), in a review of data on 17 adolescent female sex offenders, found that only 2 were involved with male co-perpetrators.

She also found that the young women in this study knew their victims and that none experienced legal consequences for their actions.

Self-report studies provide a very different view of sexual abuse perpetration and substantially increase the number of female perpetrators.

In a retrospective study of male victims, 60% reported being abused by females (Johnson and Shrier, 1987). T

The same rate was found in a sample of college students (Fritz et al., 1981).

In other studies of male university and college students, rates of female perpetration were found at levels as high as 72% to 82% (Fromuth and Burkhart, 1987, 1989; Seidner and Calhoun, 1984). Bell et al. (1981) found that 27% of males were abused by females.

In some of these types of studies, females represent as much as 50% of sexual abusers (Risin and Koss, 1987). Knopp and Lackey (1987) found that 51% of victims of female sexual abusers were male.

It is evident that case report and self-report studies yield very different types of data about prevalence.

These extraordinary differences tell us we need to start questioning all of our assumptions about perpetrators and victims of child maltreatment.

Finally, there is an alarmingly high rate of sexual abuse by females in the backgrounds of rapists, sex offenders and sexually aggressive men - 59% (Petrovich and Templer, 1984), 66% (Groth, 1979) and 80% (Briere and Smiljanich, 1993).

A strong case for the need to identify female perpetrators can be found in Table 4, which presents the findings from a study of adolescent sex offenders by O'Brien (1989).

Male adolescent sex offenders abused by "females only" chose female victims almost exclusively.

Table 4

Victim Gender Based on Who Previously Abused the Perpetrator

Gender of Perpetrators' Victimizer	Gender of Own Victim Male or Both	Female Only
Male only	67.5%	32.5%
Female only	6.7%	93.3%

Berkowitz (1993), in a Winnipeg-based study of sexually abused males in treatment groups, found the following rates of perpetration.

Table 5

Gender of Abusers of Male Victims in Treatment Groups

N %

Gender of Abusers	N	%
Intrafamilial Abuse (N=54)	54	100.0
Male perpetrated		
Female perpetrated	39	72.2

Extrafamilial Abuse (N=55)	50	90.9
Male adult		
Female adult	30	54.5
Male adolescent	39	70.9
Female adolescent	24	43.6

I Have a Special Gift for My Readers

I appreciate my readers for without them I am just another author attempting to make a difference. If my book has made a favorable impression please leave me an honest review. Thank you in advance for you participation.

My readers and I have in common a passion for the written word as well as the desire to learn and grow from books.

My special offer to you is a massive ebook library that I have compiled over the years. It contains hundreds of fiction and non-fiction ebooks in Adobe Acrobat PDF format as well as the Greek classics and old literary classics too.

In fact, this library is so massive to completely download the entire library will require over 5 GBs open on your desktop.

Use the link below and scan all of the ebooks in the library. You can select the ebooks you want individually or download the entire library.

The link below does not expire after a given time period so you are free to return for more books rather than clog your desktop. And feel free to give the link to your friends who enjoy reading too.

I thank you for reading my book and hope if you are pleased that you will leave me an honest review so that I can improve my work and or write books that appeal to your interests.

Okay, here is the link…

http://tinyurl.com/special-readers-promo

PS: If you wish to reach me personally for any reason you may simply write to mailto:support@epubwealth.com.

I answer all of my emails so rest assured I will respond.

Meet the Author

Dr. Harry Jay is Director of Research for AppliedMindSciences.com, a mental health and mind research group of Applied Web Info, and is the author of over 100 books and research papers as a behavioral scientist.

In his 32-year career, Dr. Harry Jay has contributed many new mental health treatment treatments and protocols using some of the new advances he has discovered in Energy Psychology.

He specializes in addictions of all kinds, sexual abuse, child predation and gender relationships.

He is also a board member to ePubWealth.com and serves on the science committee assisting non-fiction science writers in book publishing and promotion.

As a leading behavioral scientist, he provides profiling services to the company's ForensicsNation.com unit as well as criminal psychology research to aid in identifying and apprehending child predators and cyber-criminals of all kinds.

He resides in Southern Utah and enjoys the outdoors, fishing and photography.

Visit some of his websites
http://www.AddMeInNow.com
http://www.AppliedMindSciences.com

http://www.AppliedWebInfo.com
http://www.BookbuilderPLUS.com
http://www.BookJumping.com
http://www.EmailNations.com
http://www.EmbarrassingProblemsFix.com
http://www.ePubWealth.com
http://www.ForensicsNation.com
http://www.ForensicsNationStore.com
http://www.FreebiesNation.com
http://www.HealthFitnessWellnessNation.com
http://www.Neternatives.com
http://www.PrivacyNations.com
http://www.RetireWithoutMoney.org
http://www.SurvivalNations.com
http://www.TheBentonKitchen.com
http://www.Theolegions.org
http://www.VideoBookbuilder.com